Bernadette Fitzgerald Kay Hiatt Joyce

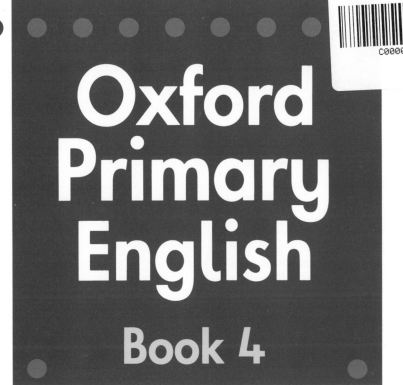

Oxford Primary English

Book 4

C000097476

Oxford University Press

Oxford University Press, Great Clarendon Street, Oxford, OX2 6DP

Oxford New York
Athens Auckland Bangkok Bogota Buenos Aires
Calcutta Cape Town Chennai Dar es Salaam Delhi
Florence Hong Kong Istanbul Karachi Kuala Lumpur
Madrid Melbourne Mexico City Mumbai Nairobi Paris
São Paulo Singapore Taipei Tokyo Toronto Warsaw

and associated companies in
Berlin Ibadan

Oxford is a trade mark of Oxford University Press

© **Bernadette Fitzgerald, Kay Hiatt and Joyce Hilyer 1993**
First published by Oxford University Press 1993
Reprinted 1994, 1998

All rights reserved. No part of this publication may be
reproduced, stored in a retrieval system, or transmitted, in
any forms or by any means, without the prior permission
in writing of Oxford University Press. Within the UK,
exceptions are allowed in respect of any fair dealing for
the purpose of research or private study, or criticism or
review, as permitted under the Copyright, Designs and
Patents Act, 1988, or in the case of reprographic reproduction
in accordance with the terms of licences issued by the
Copyright Licensing Agency. Enquiries concerning
reproduction outside those terms and in other countries
should be addressed to the Rights Department,
Oxford University Press, at the address above.

A CIP catalogue record for this book is available from
the British Library

ISBN 0 19 9165599

Typeset by Pentacor PLC, High Wycombe, Bucks.
Printed in Hong Kong

Contents

Communication

Spoken English

Aim: learning about dialects and accents.

Standard English

Standard English is the dialect or type of English spoken all around the British Isles — and by people who speak English, all around the world. It is very useful to have this one type of English which all English speakers understand.

We all need to be able to speak Standard English.

Standard English is used by newsreaders on television and radio. Someone giving a speech at a wedding would also probably use Standard English. You would probably use it when speaking to your headteacher.

Other dialects

Other dialects (types of English) are used all over the country. People in different parts of Britain may not call something by its Standard English name, but may have a different word for it in their dialect, e.g. a newt can be called an 'evet' in Cornwall, an 'asker' in parts of Wales, and, would you believe, 'tiddly-winks' in parts of Essex.

READ
WRITE

Read and copy the chart on the opposite page, and write in what the Standard English word is for the dialect word you are given. If you can, add on some more dialect words that you know, with their Standard English equivalent.

Dialect word	Region	Standard English	Picture
bosh	South Wales		
kecks	Liverpool		
loon	Aberdeen		

You might hear children or adults saying, 'We *was* late for the bus'. Although this may be correct in many local dialects, it is not Standard English. In Standard English this would be, 'We *were* late for the bus'. What has changed?

Accents around Britain

Your accent is the way you pronounce or say words. Everyone has an accent. It is often possible to guess where a person comes from because of his or her accent. People can speak Standard English using the accent of the area in which they live, e.g. Liverpool, Cardiff, Edinburgh, Dublin.

An accent survey

Keep a diary for one week. Write down in it all the different accents you hear. You might hear them:
- in the street
- at home
- on TV
- at the supermarket
- on the radio
- at the cinema.

 WRITE

Write your results in a chart like the one Hamid has started below.

Who was speaking	Where I heard it	Which accent it was
A pop star	On TV	Birmingham

Communication

Formal and informal talk

In **formal** situations we usually talk in Standard English. In **informal** situations we can choose whether to use Standard English.

Aim: learning how we talk in different ways in different situations.

In certain situations, people need to speak formally. Read what this headteacher says at her retirement ceremony.

> Ladies and Gentlemen, I would like to take this opportunity to thank you...

In other situations, the same person speaks more informally. Read what the same headteacher says when a pupil gives her a leaving present.

> Oh, thank you, Robbie!

TALK

Compare the two pictures. In what ways does the headteacher speak differently in each? Why do you think she does this?

In pairs, look closely at the two pictures on the next page. Talk about where the people are and what is happening in each picture. Discuss what you think the people in the pictures could be saying.

Think about:
• the words each person would say
• how they would say their words: politely, slowly, quietly, nervously, happily, jokingly, angrily . . .

A  **B**

TALK ▷

WRITE ▷

For each of the pictures, decide whether the talk is formal or informal.

Choose your favourite picture. Write down what the people in the picture might be saying to each other. Set it out like the script which Angus has started below:

Picture A - Conversation

Librarian (helpfully): Hello. Can I help you?

Girl (confidently): Yes please. I

WRITE ▷

Think of five people to whom you have spoken today. Write down their names and whether your talk was formal or informal, for example:

People I have spoken to today	
Name	Type of talk
My Mum	Informal

Communication

Saying the wrong thing!

Aim: learning about matching what you say to the person you're talking to.

READ

TALK

Sometimes we say the wrong thing! In the passage which follows, Karen Turpin manages to say the wrong thing to a visitor – the School Adviser. The scene takes place in a book called *Dangleboots* by Dennis Hamley. Read on with your partner to discover what happens to Karen!

The coach was to leave after lunch. The drive into the city would take about forty minutes. As they milled round the dining hall queuing for food, Andy saw the Head standing with a strange man – middle-aged, with glasses, thinning hair and wearing a brown suit.

Karen Turpin and Johnny were just in front of Andy in the queue. As they walked with their loaded trays to an empty table and Andy and Dilip started to follow them, Andy heard the Head speak to the strange man.

'You don't mind sitting with the kids, do you?'

A split-second look of stark horror crossed the stranger's face before he answered, 'No, not at all.'

'Karen.' The Head called and Karen turned.

'This is Mr Wheyfoot. He's an Adviser from the Education Authority, come to see what we do here. He'll be coming with you on the trip today. Take him to your table and keep him entertained, will you?'

Karen's face showed a look of horror even starker than that shown by Mr Wheyfoot. The Head saw it.

'Don't worry,' he said. 'Just tell him a few

of your best rude jokes. They'll keep him happy.'

Mr Wheyfoot was led to the end of the table. Karen sat at his right, Johnny next to her. Andy was opposite Karen and Dilip next to him. There was an awkward silence. Karen looked wildly from face to face. No help from anyone. Did the Head mean what he said? She cleared her throat.

'What's green and smells?' she said.

Johnny roared with laughter.

Andy was scandalized.

'You can't ask him that,' he said.

'Why not?' said Johnny.

'You know why not,' said Dilip.

'The Head told me to tell him some rude jokes,' said Karen.

'You can't tell him that one,' said Andy.

Karen thought. Then she started again.

'There was this honeymoon couple,' she said. 'And when they . . .'

Mr Wheyfoot broke in.

'I really think this conversation's gone far enough,' he said. 'I must say I'm surprised at you all.' Looking at Karen, he added, 'Especially you.'

Andy felt suddenly angry at this.

'That's not fair,' he said. 'Karen was only doing what the Head told her.'

'You couldn't have thought he was serious, surely?' said Mr Wheyfoot.

'How are we supposed to know?' said Andy. He hadn't felt so cross for a long time as he did with this peculiar person from nowhere who had been plonked down at his table. 'If a teacher tells you to do something, you've got to do it.'

'You've got a lot to learn about life,' said Mr Wheyfoot.

'You're not much help,' said Andy.

Yes, he was really surprised at just how angry he felt. That was the second time today. Anger and a wish for revenge on those who caused it.

Mr Wheyfoot raised his eyes to the ceiling.

TALK

WRITE

Pick out the wrong things which Karen says. Talk about why Karen says the wrong thing. Why do you think that the School Adviser is so shocked by what Karen says? Whose fault is it?

Write Karen's diary entry for that day – about what happened when she talked to the School Adviser. She might have started it like this:

> Monday
> I felt so cross today...

Have you ever said the wrong thing to someone? Write about what happened.

Communication

Slang

Aim: *learning about changing fashions in slang.*

READ
WRITE

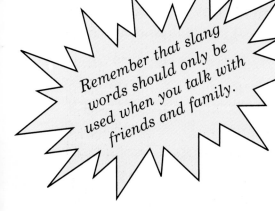

Remember that slang words should only be used when you talk with friends and family.

All change!

Look carefully at the pictures above. You will notice changing fashions in **clothes** as well as in the **slang** words these girls are using.

Here is a list of slang words used from the 1940s to the 1990s. Read them all and write down the words **you** might use with your friends.

ace	groovy	ripping
bad	lush	mint
brill	mega	spiffing
cool	neat	wicked
fab	radical	swell

Now write down a conversation you could be having with a friend in the playground. It should be about something you have both recently enjoyed very much – use some of the slang words above.

WRITE

More slang words

You could use all the slang words below to show that you don't like something or someone. Sort the words into two lists:

* slang words which you think have gone out of fashion
* slang words which are still in fashion.

chronic, corny, daft, foul, fusty, frowsy, ghastly, gross, lousy, mardy, mouldy, no good, pesky, revolting, rotten, soppy.

TALK

Look at the pictures above – now try to match the slang words below with each picture.

nut, block
mug, dial
conk, snout
gob
flaps, lugs
mits

DRAW

WRITE

Take a sheet of A4 paper, write the heading 'Slang' on it, then under the heading draw a cartoon-type character. Label him or her with the slang words above.

Communication

Written English

Aim: looking at the ways English can be written down.

READ ▷

WRITE ▷

The English you read in books, newspapers, magazines, brochures, etc. is usually written in Standard English. This is so that all the people who can read English will be able to understand it. We all need to be able to write in Standard English.

Read the texts below.

They are all written in Standard English. Why? Write your answer down.

Princess Bedelia was as lovely as the moon shining upon a lake full of water-lilies. She was as graceful as a cat leaping. And she was also extremely practical.

Bad Luck, Dead Duck

Lying there amongst the muck
Bad luck, dead duck;
Oil pollutes your river bed
How sad, too bad;
Lying still among the reeds,
Squelching mud and dead seeds,
Birds expire and fishes wheeze;
Bad luck, dead duck.

Introduction

The heart is the main organ of the body. It pumps the blood around the body. However, it can become damaged.

• Picture of a damaged heart.

Perch.

Perca fluviatilis.

A boldly coloured, handsome fish present throughout Britain in rivers, lakes, canals and ponds, and the first catch for many young anglers. Note the spiny dorsal fin for protection against predators, which include larger perch.

Size: British record: 2.523kg. For most anglers, a perch of 500gm. is a welcome capture.

READ

However, when writing down what people say we *can* use either Standard English or a local dialect. (We put what characters *say* inside speech marks.) Read the following extract from Laurie Lee's book 'Cider with Rosie'.

Laurie Goes to School

The morning came, without any warning, when my sisters surrounded me, wrapped me in scarves, tied up my bootlaces, thrust a cap on my head, and stuffed a baked potato in my pocket.

'What's this?' I said.

'You're starting school today.'

'I ain't. I'm stopping 'ome.'

'Now, come on, Loll. You're a big boy now.'

'I ain't.'

'You are.'

'Boo-hoo.'

They picked me up bodily, kicking and bawling, and carried me up to the road.

Laurie Lee
from *Cider with Rosie*

READ
WRITE

Read the questions below and write answers to them.

- Why do you think Laurie Lee chose to use some local dialect when he wrote down what Loll was saying?

- Do characters in any of your favourite stories speak in a local dialect? If so, name them.

- Do you usually write down speech in Standard English? Why?

Story

Greek myth

Aim: learning that myths are stories that offer an explanation for how things happen in the world, e.g. how the seasons change.

A myth is an ancient, traditional story of gods or heroes.

READ

'Myth' comes from 'Muthos', the Greek word for story. Some of the best known myths are those from Ancient Greece. These old tales or legends were part of the religion of the Greeks. They were handed down from generation to generation by word of mouth long before they were written down.

This is the story of Demeter and Persephone told in words and pictures.

Demeter was the goddess of corn. She possessed special powers. She made the wheat and barley ripen, the trees and plants flourish and the flowers blossom. She had a daughter called Persephone who was young and beautiful. They travelled the world together bringing in the harvests, but their favourite place on earth was the beautiful island of Sicily.

One day in Sicily Persephone wandered away from her mother to play with her friends, the nymphs. As they gathered flowers in the meadows around Mount Etna, suddenly the earth began to tremble beneath their feet and a jagged split appeared in the mountainside. As rocks and stones were hurled into the air, a dark chariot appeared drawn by black horses. It was driven by Hades, the King of the Underworld.

He saw Persephone and immediately wanted her to share his kingdom underground. He knew she would never accompany him to a land where the sun never shone, no birds sang and nothing ever grew. So before she could escape, he leant down and pulled her into his chariot and carried her down to his palace. Just as the mountainside was closing behind them, Persephone cast her girdle into the river nearby and called to the water-nymphs to carry it to her mother.

Demeter was broken-hearted when she couldn't find Persephone. She roamed the mountain slopes, calling her daughter's name. Weeks and months passed, but no one could tell her where Persephone was. She forgot her work and crops began to fail, flowers withered and died, and the fruit on the trees would not ripen.

One day as she sat wearily by a river bank, she saw something shining in the reeds. It was Persephone's golden girdle. Her heart leapt with joy. She knew that the water-nymphs must have cast it there for her to find. She set out once again, following the river upstream until she came to a waterfall and there she sat down to rest. Suddenly she heard a voice and knew the nymph of the waterfall was speaking to her. She told Demeter that when she had passed underground, she had seen Persephone sitting beside Hades on his throne. Demeter's eyes filled with tears.

She feared that she would never see her daughter again. In her grief she hid herself away in a cave and soon there was famine in the land. The starving people called to Demeter to help them but she ignored their cries.

In despair they appealed to Zeus who was king over all the gods. Demeter heard them and left her cave. She too began to beg for his help. Zeus listened. He declared that provided Persephone had eaten nothing during her stay in the underworld she could return to her mother. But if she had shared food with Hades then she must remain there for ever.

Demeter hurried down through the gateway of the underworld into the darkness until she came to the throne of Hades. There she saw her daughter with a lighted torch in her left hand and a pomegranate in her right. She reached out to claim Persephone and fetch her back to the world of the living but as she moved towards her one of the spirits of the dark cried out that Persephone had eaten six pomegranate seeds that very day. Demeter broke into a loud wailing. Her cries could be heard by the people on the earth above.

Again they called on Zeus to help. When Zeus heard what Persephone had done, he took pity on her. He agreed that for every seed she must stay a month in the underworld with Hades but for the rest of the year she could return to the surface of the earth and to her mother. And so it was from that time onwards, when Persephone is with her mother the corn ripens, the grass grows, the earth is green and it is summer. When she returns to Hades in the underworld the earth turns cold and grey and it is winter.

WRITE

Choose a part of the story that you enjoyed and write about what happened in your own words. Consider what the characters might have said to each other and write down their conversation.

Remember when you write down what someone says
- put the words which the character says inside speech marks
- start each character's words on a new line
- begin each new piece of writing with a capital letter
- finish each piece of writing with a full stop (.) or a question mark (?) or an exclamation mark (!) or a comma (,) before the final speech marks.

This is how Catherine started the conversation between Demeter and the nymph of the waterfall.

When you write down in a story the words that people say, we call it 'direct speech'.

As Demeter sat down she heard a voice calling her name.

"Demeter, Demeter, listen to me. I can help you find your daughter Persephone."

Demeter looked up to where the voice was coming from.

"Nymph of the waterfall, is that you?" she called out. "Tell me what you know."

DRAW

ACT

Do some drawings to go with your writing.

Act out the story in a small group.

Story

Modern myth

Aim: learning that myths can still be written today.

READ ▷

Ted Hughes has written a collection of stories about how creatures of the earth came to be as we know them. 'How the Whale Became' is one of these stories. It is a modern myth.

How the Whale Became

Now God had a little back-garden. In this garden he grew carrots, onions, beans and whatever else he needed for his dinner. It was a fine little garden. The plants were in neat rows, and a tidy fence kept out the animals. God was pleased with it.

One day as he was weeding the carrots he saw a strange thing between the rows. It was no more than an inch long, and it was black. It was like a black shiny bean.

At one end it had a little root going into the ground.

'That's very odd,' said God. 'I've never seen one of these before. I wonder what it will grow into.'

So he left it growing.

Next day, as he was gardening, he remembered the little shiny black thing. He went to see how it was getting on. He was surprised. During the night it had doubled its length. It was now two inches long, like a shiny black egg.

Every day God went to look at it, and every day it was bigger. Every morning, in fact, it was just twice as long as it had been the morning before.

When it was six feet long, God said:

'It's getting too big. I must pull it up and cook it.'

But he left it a day.

Next day it was twelve feet long and far too big to go into any of God's pans.

God stood scratching his head and looking at it. Already it had crushed most of his carrots out of sight. If it went on growing at this rate it would soon be pushing his house over.

Suddenly, as he looked at it, it opened an eye and looked at him.

God was amazed.

The eye was quite small and round. It was near the thickest end, and farthest from the root. He walked round to the

18

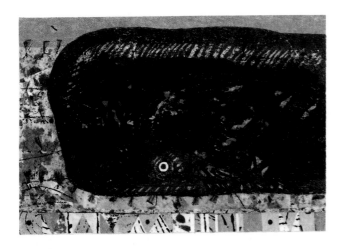

Whale-Wort.'

There was nothing God could do about that.

By next morning, Whale-Wort stretched right across the road, and his side had pushed the kitchen wall into the kitchen. He was now longer and fatter than a bus.

When God saw this, he called the creatures together.

'Here's a strange thing,' he said. 'Look at it. What are we going to do with it?'

The creatures walked round Whale-

other side, and there was another eye, also looking at him.

'Well!' said God. 'And how do you do?'

The round eye blinked, and the smooth glossy skin under it wrinkled slightly, as if the thing were smiling. But there was no mouth, so God wasn't sure.

Next morning God rose early and went out into his garden.

Sure enough, during the night his new black plant with eyes had doubled its length again. It had pushed down part of his fence, so that its head was sticking out into the road, one eye looking up it, and one down. Its side was pressed against the kitchen wall.

God walked round to its front and looked it in the eye.

'You are too big,' he said sternly. 'Please stop growing before you push my house down.'

To his surprise, the plant opened a mouth. A long slit of a mouth, which ran back on either side under the eyes.

'I can't,' said the mouth.

God didn't know what to say. At last he said:

'Well then, can you tell me what sort of a thing you are? Do you know?'

'I,' said the thing, 'am Whale-Wort. You have heard of Egg-Plant, and Buck-Wheat, and Dog-Daisy. Well, I am

Wort, looking at him. His skin was so shiny they could see their faces in it.

'Leave it,' suggested Ostrich. 'And wait till it dies down.'

'But it might go on growing,' said God. 'Until it covers the whole earth. We shall have to live on its back. Think of that.'

'I suggest,' said Mouse, 'that we throw it into the sea.'

God thought.

'No,' he said at last. 'That's too severe. Let's just leave it for a few days.'

After three more days, God's house was completely flat, and Whale-Wort was as long as a street.

'Now,' said Mouse, 'it is too late to throw it into the sea. Whale-Wort is too big to move.'

But God fastened long thick ropes round him and called up all the creatures to help haul on the ends.

'Hey!' cried Whale-Wort. 'Leave me alone.'

'You are going into the sea,' cried Mouse. 'And it serves you right. Taking up all this space.'

'But I'm happy!' cried Whale-Wort again. 'I'm happy just lying here. Leave me and let me sleep. I was made just to lie and sleep.'

'Into the sea!' cried Mouse.

'No!' cried Whale-Wort.

'Into the sea!' cried all the creatures. And they hauled on the ropes. With a great groan, Whale-Wort's root came out of the ground. He began to thresh and twist, beating down houses and trees with his long root, as the creatures dragged him willy-nilly through the countryside.

At last they got him to the top of a high cliff. With a great shout they rolled him over the edge and into the sea.

'Help! Help!' cried Whale-Wort. 'I shall drown! Please let me come back on land where I can sleep.'

'Not until you're smaller!' shouted God. 'Then you can come back.'

'But how am I to get smaller?' wept Whale-Wort, as he rolled to and fro in the sea. 'Please show me how to get smaller so that I can live on land.'

God bent down from a high cliff and poked Whale-Wort on the top of his head with his finger.

'Ow!' cried Whale-Wort. 'What was that for? You've made a hole. The water will come in.'

'No it won't,' said God. 'But some of you will come out. Now just you start

blowing some of yourself out through that hole.'

Whale-Wort blew, and a high jet of spray shot up out of the hole that God had made.

'Now go on blowing,' said God.

Whale-Wort blew and blew. Soon he was quite a bit smaller. As he shrunk, his skin, that had been so tight and glossy, became covered with tiny wrinkles. At last God said to him:

'When you're as small as a cucumber, just give a shout. Then you can come back into my garden. But until then, you shall stay in the sea.'

And God walked away with all his creatures, leaving Whale-Wort rolling and blowing in the sea.

Soon Whale-Wort was down to the size of a bus. But blowing was hard work, and by this time he felt like a sleep. He took a deep breath and sank down to the bottom of the sea for a sleep. Above all, he loved to sleep.

When he awoke he gave a roar of dismay. While he was asleep he had grown back to the length of a street and the fatness of a ship with two funnels.

He rose to the surface as fast as he could and began to blow. Soon he was back down to the size of a lorry. But soon, too, he felt like another sleep. He took a deep breath and sank to the bottom.

When he awoke he was back to the length of a street.

As fast as Whale-Wort shrinks with blowing, he grows with sleeping. Sometimes, when he is feeling very strong, he gets himself down to the size of a motor-car. But always, before he gets himself down to the size of a cucumber, he remembers how nice it is to sleep. When he wakes, he has grown again.

He longs to come back on land and sleep in the sun, with his root in the earth. But instead of that, he must roll and blow, out on the wild sea. And until he is allowed to come back on land, the creatures call him just Whale.

READ ▷
TALK ▷
WRITE ▷
DRAW ▷

Work with a partner. Talk about and write down what Ted Hughes had to know about whales in order to write the story. Decide which headings to put the information under, e.g.: appearance (what it looks like), habitat (where it lives), etc.

Still working together, make up your own modern myth. First choose an animal, an insect or a bird.
- Find out as much as you can about your creature.
- Write a story to explain how your creature got one of its special characteristics, e.g. how the fox got its bushy tail, how the hedgehog got its spines, how the elephant got its trunk.

Plan your story carefully before you start to write.

Do some drawings to go with it.

Put it in a Class Book of Modern Myths.

The language of persuasion

About the environment: photographs

Aim: learning how photographs can influence our views.

READ >
TALK >

In pairs, look at the photographs above.

- What can you see in each picture?
- What have they all got in common?
- How do these pictures make you feel?
- If a magazine or newspaper editor chose these photographs to go with an article, what do you think the article could be about?
- Why do you think the editor would choose to use photographs rather than artists' drawings?

4

5

WRITE ▷

READ ▷

Look again at each photograph and then fill in a chart like the one Amanda has started below.

Photograph number	What is in the photograph	The effect of what is happening	My feelings about it
1	Dead bird covered in oil from tanker spillage.	Kills fish and birds. Pollutes the beach.	Sad, angry, annoyed. Want to do something about it.

See if you can find more photographs like these in newspapers and magazines. Make a collection of them and add the information about them to your chart.

The language of persuasion

About the environment: magazine cover

Aim: learning how magazine covers can influence us.

READ ▷ In a small group, look at this magazine cover.

In your small group, talk about the questions below. Elect one person to make notes on your answers.

- What did you first notice when you looked at the cover?
- Look again very carefully. What else can you see?
- What do you think is the message of this cover?
- Do you think the editor has chosen a good cover for the magazine? Think and talk about:
    the choice of words
    the picture
    the lettering
    the colours.
- Why do you think there is a question on the cover?
- How does the cover make **you** feel? Has it influenced your views in any way? Give some reasons.

Look back at the photographs on pages 22 and 23. Which would you choose to put on the cover of a magazine? Give your reasons for your choice.

Now create your own magazine cover. Find a suitable picture. Think carefully about the headline or caption that you are going to write to go with it. You may like to look back at the notes you made earlier, to find out what makes a good magazine cover.

A caption is a title or a brief explanation that goes with a picture.

Look at these magazine covers. What is their message?

The language of persuasion

About the environment: letters

Aim: *learning how to write a letter to influence others.*

READ
TALK

In newspapers we often see letters which have been written by people who feel strongly about something. They hope to persuade others to agree with their point of view. Here is a letter written by a girl expressing her views about pollution. She tries to persuade her readers by giving only one side of the argument.

With a partner, read Sara's letter on the opposite page. Notice how she includes in it:

- the problem causing concern
- the reason why she is worried
- what she feels can be done about the problem – her solution.

A good way of persuading people is to give them strong reasons for agreeing with you.

When you write a formal letter, make sure that it is written in Standard English. You usually begin 'Dear Sir or Madam' and end 'Yours faithfully'.

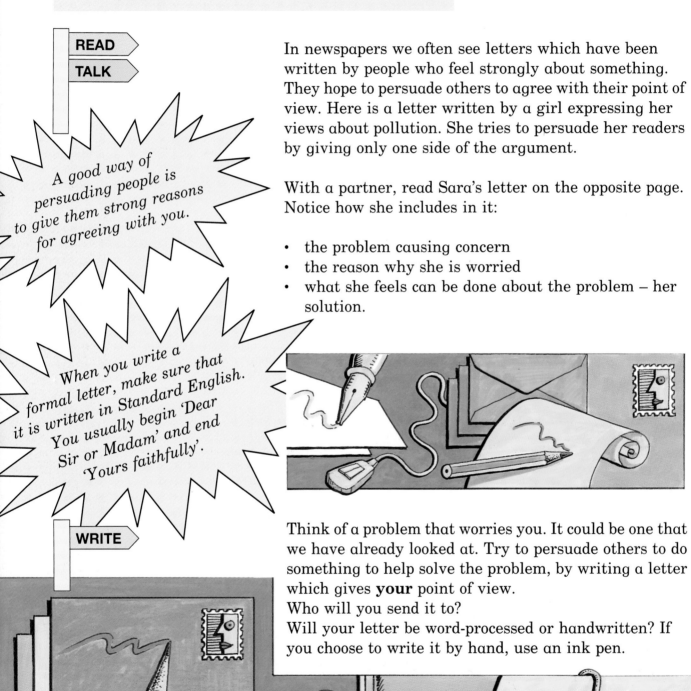

WRITE

Think of a problem that worries you. It could be one that we have already looked at. Try to persuade others to do something to help solve the problem, by writing a letter which gives **your** point of view.
Who will you send it to?
Will your letter be word-processed or handwritten? If you choose to write it by hand, use an ink pen.

Name and address
of the person to
whom the letter is
being written

Stoke Bishop CE Primary School
Cedar Park
Stoke Bishop
Bristol BS9 1BU
4 May 1993

Address of
the writer

Date

The Editor
Young Telegraph

Formal
greeting

Dear Sir or Madam,

    I am very concerned about the way our rivers
are being polluted because this is having a serious effect on the
otters in our country. They are fast disappearing.

Problem
causing
concern

Reason for
concern

    These beautiful creatures used to be seen in most parts of
Britain but now there are not so many living along our
river banks.

    Many of our rivers are badly polluted by chemicals and
these harm the otters and stop them from breeding. If we want
our otters to survive we must find out who is pouring these
chemicals into the rivers and stop them from doing it.

Solution
to problem

    Otters will become extinct unless we stop destroying their
environment. The only way of remembering them will be as
stuffed animals in museums.

Yours faithfully,
Sara Currie

Formal ending

Name of the writer

The language of persuasion

About the environment: poems

Aim: *learning how poetry can influence our views.*

The Song of the Whale

Heaving mountain in the sea,
Whale, I heard you
Grieving.

Great whale, crying for your life,
Crying for your kind, I knew
How we would use
Your dying:

Lipstick for our painted faces,
Polish for our shoes.

Tumbling mountain in the sea,
Whale, I heard you
Calling.

Bird-high notes, keening, soaring:
At their edge a tiny drum
Like a heartbeat.

We would make you
Dumb.

In the forest of the sea,
Whale, I heard you
Singing.

Singing to your kind.
We'll never let you be.
Instead of life we choose

Lipstick for our painted faces,
Polish for our shoes.

Kit Wright

Bad Luck, Dead Duck

Lying there amongst the muck
Bad luck, dead duck;
Oil pollutes your river bed
How sad, too bad;
Lying still among the reeds,
Squelching mud and dead seeds,
Birds expire and fishes wheeze;
Bad luck, dead duck.

Oil has seeped into your lungs,
Bad luck, dead duck;
A short, short life was all you had;
How sad, too bad;
Lying dead; nobody cares,
Bad luck, dead duck.

No two feet of 'Aussie' soil,
Bad luck, dead duck;
To reward you for your toil;
How sad, too bad;
As you lie between the weeds;
No one cares; no one sees;
You'll lie there for years and years;
Bad luck, dead duck.

Nicholas Davey

READ
TALK
WRITE

With a partner, read each poem aloud several times.
Now answer these questions about each poem in turn.

1 What is it about?
2 How does it make you feel?
3 Which parts of the poem make you feel like this?
(Mention particular lines, words.)
4 What do you think the writer's message is?
5 Has the poem influenced your views in any way?

Now put all your thoughts about each poem in a chart
like the one below:

Title of poem:
Name of writer:
The message of the poem:
My views have/have not been influenced by this poem because...

The language of persuasion

About people: poems

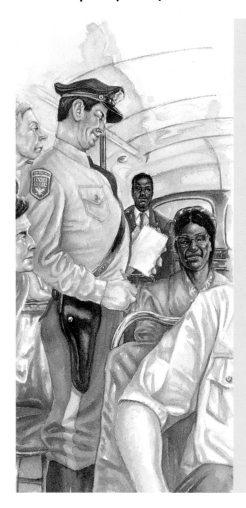

Travelling home by bus,
tired after work,
Rosa Parks –
a middle-aged black seamstress,
refused
to give up her seat to a white man.
For this
she was arrested.

This poem is about a real incident which happened on a bus in Montgomery, Alabama, in the southern area of the USA. It happened on 1 December, 1955. It is hard to believe that the law at that time said that black people had to give up their seats on a bus to any white people who were standing.

Talk together about how you will answer the following questions:

1   What is the message of the poem?
2   How does the poem make you feel?
3   Has this poem influenced your views in any way?

Now write your answers, giving your reasons.

A lament tells us about a person's deep feelings of sadness.

Not all poetry rhymes or is written in verses.

> **READ**

Read 'Shylock's Lament' aloud, with a partner.

Shylock's Lament
(from *The Merchant of Venice*)

I am a Jew. Hath not a Jew eyes? hath not a Jew hands, organs, dimensions, senses, affections, passions? fed with the same food, hurt with the same weapons, subject to the same diseases, healed by the same means, warmed and cooled by the same winter and summer as a Christian is? – if you prick us do we not bleed? if you tickle us do we not laugh? if you poison us do we not die?

William Shakespeare

> **TALK**
> **WRITE**

This passage has been taken from Act 3, Scene 1 of Shakespeare's play, *The Merchant of Venice*. This is part of a speech by Shylock, a rich moneylender. He is very upset because Antonio, another character in the play, has treated him badly.

Talk together about how you will answer the following questions:

1 How do you think the actor playing the part of Shylock would say these words?
2 In this speech, what does Shakespeare make you feel about Shylock?
3 How does Shakespeare persuade us that everyone should be treated equally well?
4 Why do you think that Shakespeare used so many questions in this speech?

Now write down your answers.

The language of persuasion

About theatre: advertisements

Aim: *learning how advertisements can persuade us to spend money.*

READ
TALK

Look closely at the advertisement on the next page and at what is written around it.

What is the purpose of this advertisement?
Where have you seen advertisements like this one?
Why do you think that advertisers choose to put their advertisements in these places?

WRITE

Complete the labelling of the 'Aladdin' advertisement. Make a list of the things you can see at the end of each numbered line. Then write your answers to the following questions:

1 Which main colours have been used in the advertisement? Why do you think that these colours have been chosen?
2 What has been chosen to go in the picture? Why?
3 Look at line 24. Why do you think that the words 'Real Panto' are used on the poster?
4 Why do you think that
   • an icecream company and
   • the Arts Council
   have sponsored this pantomime?
5 Make a list of anything unusual or funny which you can find in the poster.
6 Does the advertisement make you want to see the pantomime? Give reasons for your answer.

32

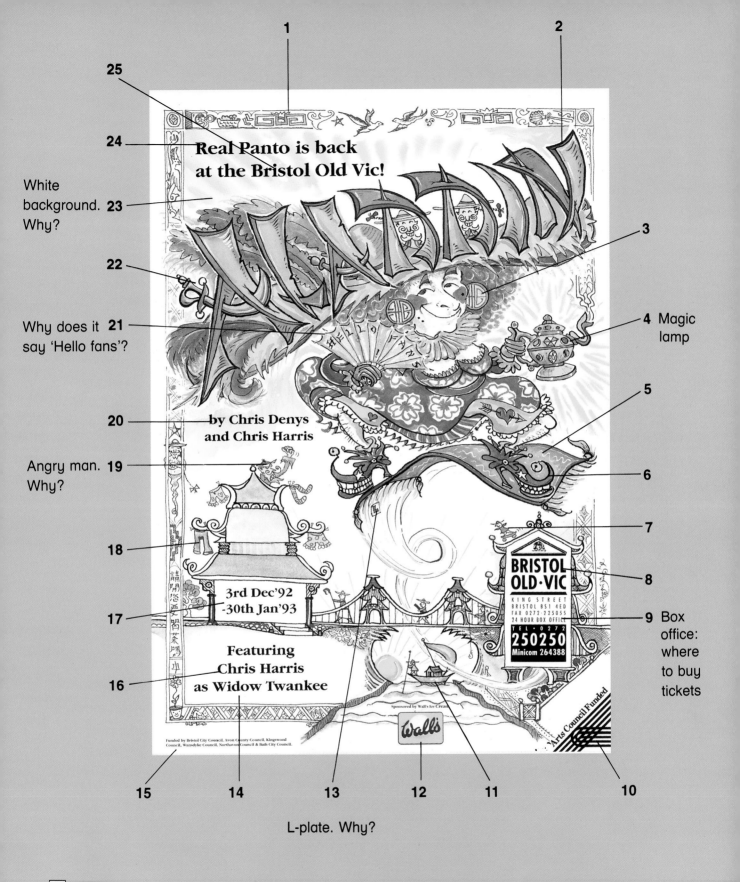

White background. 23 Why?

Why does it 21 say 'Hello fans'?

Angry man. 19 Why?

4 Magic lamp

9 Box office: where to buy tickets

L-plate. Why?

WRITE ▷

Now design a poster to advertise a play or film which you think children of your age would enjoy. Where will you display your poster?

Stereotypes

Traditional roles

Aim: learning about how princes and princesses behave in traditional stories.

TALK

WRITE

A stereotype is a commonly held view of people or individuals, e.g. all princesses are beautiful. This view is often not correct.

You will have heard and read many stories which have princes and princesses in them. Talk about them, and then write a list of the titles of as many of these traditional stories as you can remember.

Choose one of the titles which is on your list.

Think carefully about:
• what the prince and princess look like
• how they behave
• what they do in the story
• what happens to them at the end
• the clothes which they wear.

Put your information into a chart like the one on the next page which Marcia has produced. Talk about what could go into the empty boxes.

The Prince climbed the tower where the Princess

He married the beautiful

Traditional Fairy Stories	
Title	Sleeping Beauty
What the prince looks like and what he wears	Handsome, strong, white, fit, young, tall. Leather boots, velvet jacket, jewels, silk shirt, expensive clothes.
What the princess looks like and what she wears.	
What happens to the princess	
What the prince does	He cuts through bushes and thorns to rescue her – she awakes when he kisses her.
What happens at the end	

READ
TALK
WRITE

Look again at your chart and the one above. Have you written down anything that is also in Marcia's chart? Write a list of things that appear on both charts under the heading: 'Ingredients of traditional stories'.

In traditional stories, why do you think that princes and princesses are shown like this? Think about when these stories were first told and written.

The Prince slew the Dragon and rescued

The Princess was awaken by a kiss

Stereotypes
The Practical Princess

Aim: learning about how men and women can behave in a modern fairy story.

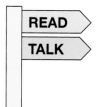
READ
TALK

Some story writers now are challenging the traditional images of princes and princesses. In these modern fairy stories princesses are not helpless: they can look after themselves!

Read aloud the short story which follows. As you read it, think about the characters of Princess Bedelia and Prince Perian – and how they behave.

The Practical Princess

Princess Bedelia was as lovely as the moon shining upon a lake full of water-lilies. She was as graceful as a cat leaping. And she was also extremely practical.

When she was born, three fairies had come to her cradle to give her gifts as was usual in that country. The first fairy had given her beauty. The second had given her grace. But the third, who was a wise old creature, had said, 'I give her common sense.'

'I don't think much of that gift,' said King Ludwig, raising his eyebrows. 'What good is common sense to a princess? All she needs is charm.'

Nevertheless, when Bedelia was eighteen years old, something happened which made the king change his mind.

A dragon moved into the neighbourhood. He settled in a dark cave on top of a mountain, and the first thing he did was to send a message to the king. 'I must have a princess to devour,' the message said, 'or I shall breathe out my fiery breath and destroy the kingdom.'

Sadly, King Ludwig called together his councillors and read them the message. 'Perhaps,' said the Prime Minister, 'we had better advertise for a knight to slay the dragon? That is what is generally done in these cases.'

'I'm afraid we haven't time,' answered the king. 'The dragon has only given us until tomorrow morning. There is no help for it. We shall have to send him the princess.'

Princess Bedelia had come to the meeting because, as she said, she liked to mind her own business and this was certainly her business.

'Rubbish!' she said. 'Dragons can't tell the difference between princesses and anyone else. Use your common sense. He's just asking for me because he's a snob.'

'That may be so,' said her father, 'but if we don't send you along, he'll destroy the kingdom.'

'Right!' said Bedelia. 'I see I'll have to deal with this myself.' She left the council chamber. She got the largest and gaudiest of her state robes and stuffed it with straw,

and tied it together with string. Into the centre of the bundle she packed about fifty kilos of gunpowder. She got two strong young men to carry it up the mountain for her. She stood in front of the dragon's cave, and called, 'Come out! Here's the princess!'

The dragon came blinking and peering out of the darkness. Seeing the bright robe covered with gold and silver embroidery, and hearing Bedelia's voice, he opened his mouth wide.

At Bedelia's signal, the two young men swung the robe and gave it a good heave, right down the dragon's throat. Bedelia threw herself flat on the ground, and the two young men ran.

As the gunpowder met the flames inside the dragon, there was a tremendous explosion.

Bedelia got up, dusting herself off. 'Dragons,' she said, 'are not very bright.'

She left the two young men sweeping up the pieces, and she went back to the castle to have her geography lesson.

The lesson that morning was local geography. 'Our kingdom, Arapathia, is bounded on the north by Istven,' said the

teacher. 'Lord Garp, the ruler of Istven, is old, crafty, rich, and greedy.' At that very moment, Lord Garp of Istven was arriving at the castle. Word of Bedelia's destruction of the dragon had reached him. 'That girl,' said he, 'is just the wife for me.' And he had come with a hundred finely-dressed courtiers and many presents to ask King Ludwig for her hand.

The king sent for Bedelia. 'My dear,' he said, clearing his throat nervously, 'just see who is here.'

'I see. It's Lord Garp,' said Bedelia. She turned to go.

'He wants to marry you,' said the king.

Bedelia looked at Lord Garp. His face was like an old napkin, crumpled and wrinkled. It was covered with warts, as if someone had left crumbs on the napkin. He had only two teeth. Six long hairs grew from his chin, and none on his head. She felt like screaming.

However, she said, 'I'm very flattered. Thank you, Lord Garp. Just let me talk to my father in private for a minute.' When they had retired to a small room behind the throne, Bedelia said to the king, 'What will

Lord Garp do if I refuse to marry him?'

'He is rich, greedy, and crafty,' said the king unhappily. 'He is also used to having his own way in everything. He will be insulted. He will probably declare war on us, and then there will be trouble.'

'Very well,' said Bedelia. 'We must be practical.'

She returned to the throne room. Smiling sweetly at Lord Garp, she said, 'My lord, as you know, it is customary for a princess to set tasks for anyone who wishes to marry her. Surely you wouldn't like me to break the custom. And you are bold and powerful enough, I know, to perform any task.'

'That is true,' said Lord Garp smugly, stroking the six hairs on his chin. 'Name your task.'

'Bring me,' said Bedelia, 'a branch from the Jewel Tree of Paxis.'

Lord Garp bowed, and off he went. 'I think,' said Bedelia to her father, 'that we have seen the last of him. For Paxis is fifteen hundred kilometres away, and the Jewel Tree is guarded by lions, serpents, and wolves.'

But in two weeks, Lord Garp was back.

With him he bore a chest, and from the chest he took a wonderful twig. Its bark was of rough gold. The leaves that grew from it were of fine silver. The twig was covered with blossoms, and each blossom had petals of mother-of-pearl and centres of sapphires, the colour of the evening sky.

Bedelia's heart sank as she took the twig. But then she said to herself, 'Use your common sense, my girl! Lord Garp never travelled three thousand kilometres in two weeks, nor is he the man to fight his way through lions, serpents, and wolves.'

She looked carefully at the branch. Then she said, 'My lord, you know that the Jewel Tree of Paxis is a living tree, although it is made of jewels.'

'Why, of course,' said Lord Garp. 'Everyone knows that.'

'Well,' said Bedelia, 'then why is it that these blossoms have no scent?'

Lord Garp turned red.

'I think,' Bedelia went on, 'that this branch was made by the jewellers of Istven, who are the best in the world. Not very nice of you, my lord. Some people might even call it cheating.'

Lord Garp shrugged. He was too old and rich to feel ashamed. But like many men used to having their own way, the more Bedelia refused him, the more he was determined to have her.

'Never mind all that,' he said. 'Set me another task. This time, I swear I will perform it.'

Bedelia sighed. 'Very well. Then bring me a cloak made from the skins of the salamanders who live in the Volcano of Scoria.'

Lord Garp bowed, and off he went. 'The Volcano of Scoria,' said Bedelia to her father, 'is covered with red-hot lava. It burns steadily with great flames, and pours out poisonous smoke so that no one can come within a kilometre of it.'

'You have certainly profited by your geography lessons,' said the king, with admiration.

Nevertheless, in a week, Lord Garp was back. This time, he carried a cloak that shone and rippled like all the colours of fire. It was made of scaly skins, stitched together with golden wire as fine as a hair; and each scale was red and orange and blue, like a tiny flame.

Bedelia took the splendid cloak. She said to herself, 'Use your head, miss! Lord Garp never climbed the red-hot slopes of the Volcano of Scoria.'

A fire was burning in the fireplace of the throne room. Bedelia hurled the cloak into it. The skins blazed up in a flash, blackened, and fell to ashes.

Lord Garp's mouth fell open. Before he could speak, Bedelia said, 'That cloak was a fake, my lord. The skins of salamanders who can live in the Volcano of Scoria wouldn't burn in a little fire like that one.'

Lord Garp turned pale with anger. He hopped up and down, unable at first to do anything but splutter.

'Ub-ub-ub!' he cried. Then, controlling himself, he said, 'So be it. If I can't have you, no one shall!'

He pointed a long, skinny finger at her. On the finger was a magic ring. At once, a great wind arose. It blew through the throne room. It sent King Ludwig flying one way and his guards the other. It picked up Bedelia and whisked her off through the air. When she could catch her breath and look about her, she found herself in a room at the top of a tower.

Bedelia peered out of the window. About the tower stretched an empty, barren plain. As she watched, a speck appeared in the distance. A plume of dust rose behind it. It drew nearer and became Lord Garp on horseback.

He rode to the tower and looked up at Bedelia. 'Aha!' he croaked. 'So you are safe

and snug, are you? And will you marry me now?'

'Never,' said Bedelia, firmly.

'Then stay there until never comes,' snarled Lord Garp.

Away he rode.

For the next two days, Bedelia felt very sorry for herself. She sat wistfully by the window, looking out at the empty plain. When she was hungry, food appeared on the table. When she was tired, she lay down on the narrow cot and slept. Each day, Lord Garp rode by and asked if she had changed her mind, and each day she refused him. Her only hope was that, as so often happens in old tales, a prince might come riding by who would rescue her.

But on the third day, she gave herself a shake.

'Now then, pull yourself together,' she said sternly. 'If you sit waiting for a prince to rescue you, you may sit here forever. Be practical! If there's any rescuing to be done,

you're going to have to do it yourself.'

She jumped up. There was something she had not yet done, and now she did it. She tried the door.

It opened.

Outside, were three other doors. But there was no sign of a staircase, or any way down from the top of the tower.

She opened two of the doors and found that they led into cells just like hers, but empty.

Behind the fourth door, however, lay what appeared to be a haystack.

From beneath it came the sound of snores. And between snores, a voice said, 'Sixteen million and twelve . . . *snore* . . . sixteen million and thirteen . . . *snore* . . . sixteen million and fourteen . . .'

Cautiously, she went closer. Then she saw that what she had taken for a haystack was in fact an immense pile of blonde hair. Parting it, she found a young man, sound asleep.

As she stared, he opened his eyes. He blinked at her. 'Who –?' he said. Then he said, 'Sixteen million and fifteen,' closed his eyes, and fell asleep again.

Bedelia took him by the shoulder and shook him hard. He awoke, yawning, and tried to sit up. But the mass of hair made this difficult.

'What on earth is the matter with you?' Bedelia asked. 'Who are you?'

'I am Prince Perian,' he replied, 'the rightful ruler of – oh dear! Here I go again. Sixteen million and . . .' His eyes began to close.

Bedelia shook him again. He made a violent effort and managed to wake up enough to continue, '– of Istven. But Lord Garp has put me under a spell. I have to count sheep jumping over a fence, and this puts me to slee-ee-ee–'

He began to snore lightly.

'Dear me,' said Bedelia. 'I must do something.'

She thought hard. Then she pinched Perian's ear, and this woke him with a start. 'Listen,' she said. 'It's quite simple. It's all in your mind, you see. You are imagining the sheep jumping over the fence – no! Don't go to sleep again!

'This is what you must do. Imagine them jumping backwards. As you do, *count* them backwards, and when you get to *one*, you'll be wide awake.'

The prince's eyes snapped open. 'Marvellous!' he said. 'Will it work?'

'It's bound to,' said Bedelia. 'For if the sheep going one way will put you to sleep, their going back again will wake you up.'

Hastily, the prince began to count, 'Sixteen million and fourteen, sixteen million and thirteen, sixteen million and twelve . . .'

'Oh, my goodness,' cried Bedelia, 'count by hundreds, or you'll never get there.'

He began to gabble as fast as he could, and with each moment that passed, his eyes sparkled more brightly, his face grew

livelier, and he seemed a little stronger, until at last he shouted, 'Five, four, three, two, ONE!' and awoke completely.

He struggled to his feet, with a little help from Bedelia.

'Heavens!' he said. 'Look how my hair and beard have grown. I've been here for years. Thank you, my dear. Who are you, and what are you doing here?'

Bedelia quickly explained.

Perian shook his head. 'One more crime of Lord Garp's,' he said. 'We must escape and see that he is punished.'

'Easier said than done,' Bedelia replied. 'There are no stairs in this tower, as far as I can tell, and the outside wall is much too smooth to climb.'

Perian frowned. 'This will take some thought,' he said. 'What we need is a long rope.'

'Use your common sense,' said Bedelia. 'We haven't any rope.'

Then her face brightened, and she clapped her hands. 'But we have your beard,' she laughed.

Perian understood at once, and chuckled. 'I'm sure it will reach almost to the ground,' he said. 'But we haven't any scissors to cut it off with.'

'That is so,' said Bedelia. 'Hang it out of the window and let me climb down. I'll search the tower and perhaps I can find a ladder, or a hidden staircase. If all else fails, I can go for help.'

She and the prince gathered up great armfuls of the beard and staggered into Bedelia's room, which had the largest window. The prince's long hair trailed behind and nearly tripped him.

He threw the beard out of the window, and sure enough the end of it came to within a metre of the ground.

Perian braced himself, holding the beard with both hands to ease the pull on his chin.

Bedelia climbed out of the window and slid down the beard. She dropped to the ground and sat for a moment, breathless.

And as she sat there, out of the wilderness came the drumming of hoofs, a cloud of dust, and then Lord Garp on his swift horse.

With one glance, he saw what was happening. He shook his fist up at Prince Perian.

'Meddlesome fool!' he shouted. 'I'll teach you to interfere.'

He leaped from the horse and grabbed the beard. He gave it a tremendous yank. Head-first came Perian, out of the window. Down he fell, and with a thump, he landed right on top of old Lord Garp.

This saved Perian, who was not hurt at all. But it was the end of Lord Garp.

Perian and Bedelia rode back to Istven on Lord Garp's horse.

In the great city, the prince was greeted with cheers of joy – once everyone had recognized him after so many years and under so much hair.

And of course, since Bedelia had rescued him from captivity, she married him. First, however, she made him get a haircut and a shave so that she could see what he really looked like.

For she was always practical.

TALK

WRITE

Did you enjoy the story of 'The Practical Princess'? Discuss it with your partner, then write down what you thought about it.

Can you remember which gift the third fairy gave to Princess Bedelia? If you could give a modern baby girl any gift, magical or real, what would you give her? Write an explanation of why you chose that gift and what you hope the girl would be able to do with it.

Now re-read the story.

READ

WRITE

DRAW

Write a list of ways in which this story is different from a traditional fairy story.

Newspaper report

Now, imagine that you are a newspaper reporter. You went up the mountain with Princess Bedelia and the two young men who were carrying the dummy to trick the dragon. Before you write your report for the front page of the Arapathia daily newspaper,
- read this part of the story again
- write notes on the main points which you will include in your article.

Remember to:
- give your report an eye-catching headline
- write in columns rather than across the page
- give some of your paragraphs sub-headings
- give your newspaper a name, a date and a price
- include an illustration.

You may be able to draft and publish your report on a word processor.

Advertisement

Write the advertisement which King Ludwig did not have time to write – for a knight to slay the dragon. Plan carefully how you will lay it out and present it.

Here is a classified advertisement based on a traditional story. Can you tell which one?

BEANS BEANS BEANS For overnight success, plant now. Good climbers, £1.50. Giant optional.

45

Language in action

Language wall

Aim: learning about why you use language.

READ
TALK
WRITE

You know a lot about language already. You use it every time you read, write, speak and listen. You may be lucky enough to know more than one language.

Brainstorm on a large sheet of paper your ideas about these questions:

What is language?

Why do you need to use language?

Where do you see language?

Where do you hear language?

READ
WRITE

Language wall

How to build a language wall:

- Choose a coloured piece of A4 paper.
- Decide what you want to write in a sentence about language on your piece of paper. Each sheet of paper will be like a brick in the wall.
- Start your sentence like this:
  I use language to . . .
  or like this:
  Language is . . .
- If you can write it in more than one language, do so on your brick.
- Make your writing big and bright so that other people can read it from a distance.
- Decorate your brick in any way you choose.
- When you are pleased with your brick, decide where you want to put it on the wall.
- Do as many bricks as you can.

Language in action

Insults

Aim: learning how characters in two of Shakespeare's plays use language to insult each other.

READ
TALK
ACT

Read aloud and act out these short extracts from two of Shakespeare's plays. Think carefully about how these angry characters might sound, look, stand, and move.

A Midsummer Night's Dream

In the middle of this play, two girls (Helena and Hermia) argue and insult each other because they are both in love with the same boy. Here are some of the names which they call each other:

Helena	Injurious Hermia! Most ungrateful maid!
Hermia	*(to Helena)* You juggler, you canker-blossom, You thief of love!
Helena	*(to Hermia)* You counterfeit, you puppet you!
Hermia	*(to Helena)* Thou painted maypole.
Helena	*(about Hermia)* She was a vixen when she went to school.

READ
TALK
ACT

Romeo and Juliet

In this play set in Italy, two neighbouring families (the Montagues and the Capulets) hate each other. One hot afternoon, the men connected with the two families shout these insults at each other. Act them out in your group.

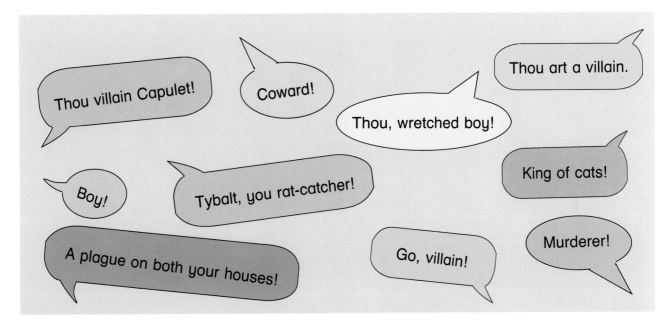

TALK

Talk about the choice of words which the characters use to insult each other in both extracts. Which insults do the characters use which you could still hear said today?

Talk about times:
*   when you have called people names
*   when other people have called you names
*   when you have heard people calling each other names.

How do you feel if people call you names?

WRITE

There is an old saying which you still hear people using today:

*Sticks and stones may break my bones
But words will never hurt me!*

Write down your feelings about name-calling in any way you choose.

Poetry

Ballad

Aim: learning that you can tell a story in a poem.

Like other stories, ballads have an opening, setting, characters, and a plot.

READ

TALK

Ballads are poems that tell a story. Long ago, ballads were not written down. They were recited or sung by travelling minstrels. Since then they have been collected and printed. In later centuries, poets like Robert Southey, who lived from 1774 to 1843, have made up their own ballads.

In a small group, take it in turns to read aloud together Robert Southey's ballad 'The Inchcape Rock'.

The Inchcape Rock

No stir in the air, no stir in the sea,
The ship was as still as she could be,
Her sails from heaven received no motion,
Her keel was steady in the ocean.

Without either sign or sound of their shock
The waves flow'd o'er the Inchcape Rock;
So little they rose, so little they fell,
They did not move the Inchcape Bell.

The good old Abbot of Aberbrothok
Had placed that bell on the Inchcape Rock;
On a buoy in the storm it floated and swung,
And over the waves its warning rung.

When the rock was hid by the surge's swell,
The mariners heard the warning bell;
And then they knew the perilous Rock,
And blessed the Abbot of Aberbrothok.

The sun in heaven was shining gay,
All things were joyful on that day;
The sea-birds screamed as they wheeled round,
And there was joyance in their sound.

The buoy of the Inchcape Bell was seen
A darker speck on the ocean green;
Sir Ralph the Rover walked his deck,
And he fixed his eye on the darker speck.

He felt the cheering power of spring,
It made him whistle, it made him sing;
His heart was mirthful to excess,
But the Rover's mirth was wickedness.

His eye was on the Inchcape float;
Quoth he, 'My men, put out the boat,
And row me to the Inchcape Rock,
And I'll plague the priest of Aberbrothok.'

The boat is lowered, the boatmen row,
And to the Inchcape Rock they go;
Sir Ralph bent over from the boat
And he cut the bell of the Inchcape float.

Down sank the bell, with a gurgling sound,
The bubbles rose and burst around;
Quoth Sir Ralph, 'The next who comes to the Rock
Won't bless the Abbot of Aberbrothok.'

Sir Ralph the Rover sailed away,
He scoured the seas for many a day;
And now grown rich with plundered store,
He steers his course for Scotland's shore.

So thick a haze o'erspreads the sky
They cannot see the sun on high;
The wind hath blown a gale all day,
At evening it hath died away.

On the deck the Rover takes his stand,
So dark it is they see no land.
Quoth Sir Ralph, 'It will be lighter soon,
For there is the dawn of the rising moon.'

'Canst hear,' said one, 'the breakers roar?
For methinks we should be near the shore;
Now where we are I cannot tell,
But I wish I could hear the Inchcape Bell.'

They hear no sound, the swell is strong;
Though the wind hath fallen, they drift along,
Till the vessel strikes with a shivering shock;
Cried they, 'It is the Inchcape Rock!'

Sir Ralph the Rover tore his hair,
He cursed himself in his despair;
The waves rush in on every side,
The ship is sinking beneath the tide,

But even in his dying fear
One dreadful sound could the Rover hear,
A sound as if with the Inchcape Bell,
The fiends below were ringing his knell.

Robert Southey

WRITE
READ
TALK

Did you enjoy the poem? Write down what you thought about it.

Now read the poem aloud once again. Put as much expression into your voice as you can. Then sit quietly for a moment.

- What pictures did you see in your mind as you heard the poem?
- Were there any words that you especially liked?
- Describe the setting at the beginning of the poem (verses 1 and 2).
- What kind of person was the Abbot of Aberbrothok?
- Do you think Sir Ralph deserved what happened to him at the end of the poem? Say why.
- What did you think of the last verse? Is it a good ending to the poem?

Ballads have a strong rhythm and a regular rhyme.

WRITE
DRAW

Imagine that you are one of the ship's survivors. Fill in the ship's log about what happened. This could be one of the last entries:

2ⁿᵈ October We are getting close to the Scottish shore. All the crew are happy to be nearly home. We have had two days of fog when not a sail could be seen.

Either write a newspaper story on the sinking of the pirate ship (the information on page 78 will help you) **or** write a story of 'The Inchcape Rock' in your own words, as a book to go in the library.

Choose your favourite verse or verses. Copy them out in your best handwriting and illustrate them.

A newspaper article contains facts, and is written to grab the reader's attention.

Non-fiction texts in our lives

Allsorts

Aim: finding out about writing which has my name on it.

READ

An autobiography is the story of a person's life written by that person.

Samantha and her class were writing their autobiographies. Their teacher had asked them to bring in texts that were important to them, and that had their names on them. These are the texts that Samantha brought in to show her partner.

A NEWTOWN CENTRAL SWIMMING CLUB GALA 1992 Second · 100 metres crawl Samantha Morrison. signed C Crabtree

B SAMANTHA MORRISON 14·50 8·1·82

C CYCLING PROFICIENCY AWARD SAMANTHA MORRISON DATE 30·4·89 SIGNED Gill Mayne

D JUNIOR DRAMA GROUP · MS. HULL WEST NEWTOWN DRAMA THE CACTUS CLUB · 52 MAYBE AV NEWTOWN · YORKSHIRE HD9 1B2 0484 872115 Samantha Morrison MEMBERSHIP No 425 VALID UNTIL 2.9.91

E Confidential PRIVATE KEEP OUT! SAMMY'S DIARY

F Wednesday POST CARD
Dear Sammy
You won't believe how wet it is here. I think I'm growing webbed feet! We've been to the cinema five times now, and been ten pin bowling twice. Really do wish you were here. Dave sends his love. Yesterday we went bird watching (in the rain, of course) saw waders and gulls. Hope Tomas is behaving.
bye for now Annie x
Ms. S. Morrison
25 North Street
Newtown
Yorkshire
HD4 3DD

G Happy birthday 1 today HONEY have a wonderful time

WRITE

For each text, decide on

- what it is
- why it was written
- who would read it.

Fill in your information on a chart like the one Samantha has started:

Picture	Form (what is it?)	Purpose (why was it written?)	Audience (Who will read it?)
A	Swimming award.	To tell people that I came second in the gala.	Myself, my family, my teachers.

Now write a list of texts that are important to you, and that have your name on them.

Non-fiction texts in our lives

Birthday cards

Aim: *learning about different types of birthday cards.*

READ

Read the front of this birthday card with a partner.

TALK

WRITE

Is it anything like the birthday cards which you have received?

- Do you think that an eight year old would like this card? Write down your reasons.
- What do you think of the colours used, and the illustrations?
- There are several different types of jokes on this comic-style birthday card. Pick two different types and write an example of each.
- Why do you think the artist has put graffiti on the card?

READ

Read carefully the front cover and inside of the birthday card below:

Can you help the alien find the right path back to his spaceship!

WRITE

- Why do you think that the designer has included a puzzle in the birthday card?
- Do you think that an eight year old would like this card? Say why.
- Can you find any links between the cover of the card and the puzzle page? Say what they are.

Look carefully at the front of this card. Talk with your partner about what you can see.

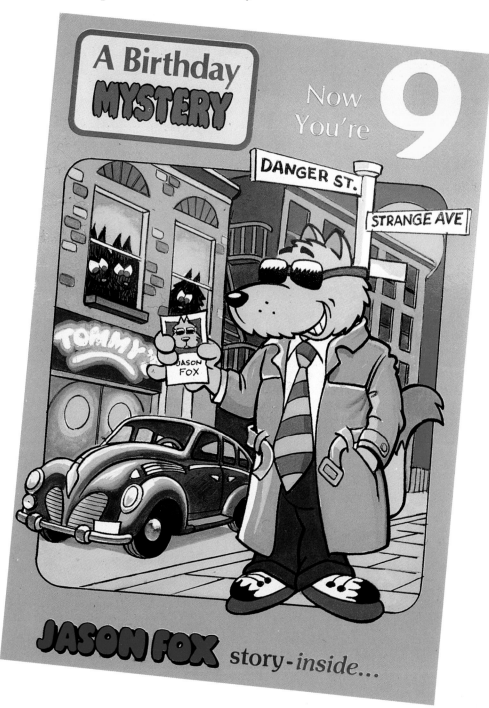

How has the designer tried to make the front of the card interesting to a nine year old child? Look at:
* the character
* the background
* the colours
* the words.

READ >
TALK >

In pairs, read the story which was inside this birthday card, and say what you think of it.

JASON FOX and the STOLEN SAUSAGES

Jason Fox our ace super sleuth has been called in by Police Chief O'Rourk.

'The Doggie Diner Cafe has been robbed and the crooks have taken all the sausages', said O'Rourk. 'This looks like the work of Hot Dog Hermon and his gang' replied Jason, 'they love sausages — I'll check out Tommy's Pad, that's where they hang out!'

Jason's dark glasses looked really cool — but wearing them he couldn't see the three pairs of evil eyes watching him from a window over Tommy's Pad.

Soon our hero was captured by Hot Dog Hermon and his gang. Jason was locked in a small upstairs room with only a bed, a window and on the floor the string of stolen sausages. Can you guess how our cool super-sleuth managed to escape?

Answer:
He tied one end of the string of sausages to the leg of the bed and lowered the other end out of the window and escaped climbing down on them.

WRITE >
DRAW >

Make your own!

Now, design and write a story birthday card of your own. Think who you will give your card to on his or her birthday – what kind of story would they like? Will it be an adventure, a mystery, science fiction, or another kind of story? Write your story in no more than 160 words.

Non-fiction texts in our lives

Diaries

Aim: learning how people write in diaries.

Many people keep a private diary in which they record the day-to-day events of their lives. Have you got one? One famous diarist, called Samuel Pepys, lived in the 17th century. He wrote his diary in a code so that no one else would be able to read it. This is what the code looked like:

Over 150 years after he died, the code was deciphered and his diary was published.

As well as writing about himself, Pepys put in his diary lots of facts about what was happening in his city. He gave vivid eyewitness accounts of famous events like the Plague and the Great Fire of London. This is how he described the fire:

Everybody endeavouring to remove their goods, and flinging into the river or bringing them into lighters that lay off; poor people staying in their houses as long as till the very fire touched them, and then running into boats, or clambering from one pair of stairs by the water-side to another. And among other things the poor pigeons . . . were loath to leave their houses, but hovered about the windows and balconies till they . . . burned their wings and fell down.

(*Lighters* are flat-bottomed boats.)

WRITE

Write a diary entry for one of the following: a special day at school, a memorable weekend, a school trip.
Include what happens to you and any special events going on.

Edith Holden chose to write about nature in her diary. She kept a nature diary for the year 1906. In it she described and painted the wildlife that surrounded her home in the country. This is a page from her diary.

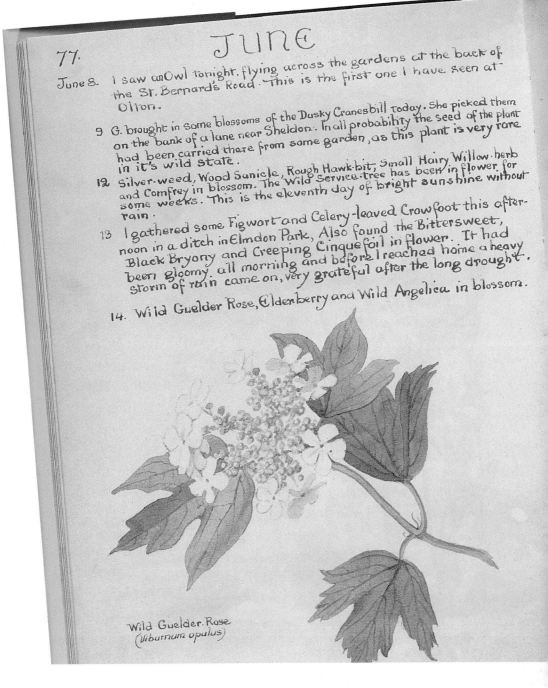

JUNE

77.

June 8. I saw an Owl tonight, flying across the gardens at the back of the St. Bernard's Road. This is the first one I have seen at Olton.

9 G. brought in some blossoms of the Dusky Cranesbill today. She picked them on the bank of a lane near Sheldon. In all probability the seed of the plant had been carried there from some garden, as this plant is very rare in it's wild state.

12 Silver-weed, Wood Sanicle, Rough Hawk-bit, Small Hairy Willow-herb and Comfrey in blossom. The Wild Service-tree has been in flower for some weeks. This is the eleventh day of bright sunshine without rain.

13 I gathered some Figwort and Celery-leaved Crowfoot this afternoon in a ditch in Elmdon Park, Also found the Bittersweet, Black Bryony and Creeping Cinquefoil in flower. It had been gloomy all morning and before I reached home a heavy storm of rain came on, very grateful after the long drought.

14. Wild Guelder Rose, Elderberry and Wild Angelica in blossom.

Wild Guelder Rose
(Viburnum opulus)

Keep your own nature diary for one day or one week. Mention the weather, plants, animals, and birds, and include some drawings to go with your writing.

Why do you think people choose to write diaries?

You can write a diary imagining that you are a character in a story or a character in history. Jessica wrote a diary pretending that she was Pip in the story by Charles Dickens called *Great Expectations*. In the story, the young boy Pip visited the graveyard where his family was buried.

24th December

This afternoon as it was getting dusk, I stumbled through the marshes towards the graveyard where most of my kin is buried. As I sat and gazed at their tombstones, all of a sudden I heard a terrible voice from behind my shoulder demanding to know my name. A dark silhouette of a figure emerged from behind a tombstone. A terrible figure – torn by brambles, stained by berries, stung by nettles, and smothered in mud, who had been soaked in water and who carried an iron on his leg which he shifted around uncomfortably.

I told him my name was Pip, and when he asked me where I lived I pointed to the far side of the river where our small village lay.

He caught my legs, turned me upside down and shook me hard for any treasures to spill from my pockets. The only thing that fell out was a stale bread crust. He perched me on a tombstone as he ate the bread ravenously and demanded to know about my mother and father. When I pointed to the grave, the man seemed worried. I told him that my sister's husband Joe was a blacksmith and he gazed at his leg and then tilted me back and made me promise to get him a file and some food. I said I would get him what he wanted and meet him at the Battery early in the morning.

Away the fearful man went, not daring to look down at the graves in case the dead reached out and dragged him down. He stiffly clambered over the church wall and went on again towards the river. As he picked his way among the great stepping stones, for a second I was sorrowful for him. Then I grew frightened and I ran home without stopping.

Choose a character in a story or a character from history. Write a diary entry imagining that you are that character.

The purpose of some diaries is to amuse. Read the diary below:

The Hamster's Diary

11 p.m.	Wake up.
11.30 p.m.	Get out of bed.
Midnight	Walk around cage.
1 a.m.	Eat breakfast (nuts again).
2 a.m.	Re-arrange sawdust.
3 a.m.	Start jogging on wheel.
4 a.m.	Still jogging on wheel (needs oiling).
4.30 a.m.	Soon be fit enough for London Marathon (hamster section).
5 a.m.	Large human crashes downstairs, switches on bright lights. Human rattles cage and shouts. He is wearing striped suit tied with string.
7 a.m.	Feeling tired, get into bed.
7.30 a.m.	Large and small humans come downstairs. They shout, play music, punish eggs in boiling water and cut bread up with a knife.
9 a.m.	Humans disappear. Peace. Sleep.

Martyn Wiley

 TALK WRITE

Talk with a partner about how this diary is different from the other diaries you have read.

Write a diary entry as if you were an animal – it could be your pet or a different animal that you know about. Do some drawings to go with your writing.

Presenting information

Information booklet

> **Aim:** *learning how to gather and present information in a booklet.*

READ
WRITE

Collecting information

Tim wanted to write an information booklet on the causes of heart disease, as part of his 'Healthy Living' topic.

He began by writing down 'Heart Disease.'

1 Which topic are you studying at the moment? Is there a part of it that you could write a booklet on? Write down the name of that part. This will be the subject of your booklet.

Tim wrote down what he already knew about the causes of heart disease.

2 Write down what you already know about your subject.

Next Tim listed some questions to which he wanted to find answers.

3 Write some questions about your subject to which you would like to find answers.

Then Tim thought about *where* he would find his information, e.g. from people, magazines, books, databases . . .

4 Write down where you might find your information.

Tim collected his information.

5 Now, like Tim, collect your information.

READ

Once he had made notes about Heart Disease, Tim followed the guide below in order to produce his information booklet. Read it through carefully.

1　Think about who will read your booklet.

2　Read all your notes through again.

3　Sort your notes into sections.

4　Give each section a heading.

5　Using your notes to help you, write your information in your own words, under each heading.

6　Decide how to help your reader by adding
  * labelled diagrams
  * charts
  * pictures
  * graphs.
  Do not draw them now – just make a note about what you will use.

7　Use your headings as a contents list.

8　Decide on
  * the size of your booklet
  * the shape
  * the colour of the paper you will use
  * the number of pages.

9　Choose a title for your booklet.

Turn over and see how Tim planned and produced his booklet. You can do the same with your information.

After reading the guide, Tim planned his leaflet. He had already decided to produce his booklet for ten and eleven year olds. Read what he wrote as he was planning his pages.

Introduction

The heart is the main organ of the body. It pumps the blood around the body. However, it can become damaged.

• Picture of a damaged heart.

Eating Fat

Fat is one of the main risk factors in causing heart attacks. If a lot of fat is eaten the arteries may clog up with fat. The blood will not flow properly and a heart attack may happen.

• Picture of a clogged-up artery.

Exercise

Lack of exercise may cause a heart attack. Being active is not only good for the circulation and heart, it also uses lots of calories and helps people lose weight.

• Picture of a man in jogging kit on weighing scales.

Fat-who needs it?

LOOK AFTER YOURSELF!

guide to HEALTHY EATING

LOOK AFTER YOUR HEART

EXERCISE. WHY BOTHER?

A simple guide to getting fitter for adults of all ages

SPORTS COUNCIL

FREE! INCLUDES RECIPES

FOOD FOR THE HEART

FOOD FOR THE HEART
A Health Education Authority Promotion

LOOK AFTER YOUR HEART

Contents

Introduction
Eating Fat
Exercise
Good Foods
Bad Foods

Information is usually written in the present tense.

Good Foods

• Pictures of a carrot, an apple and a cauliflower.

Bad Foods

• Pictures of ice cream, chips, salt, chocolate.

READ

Tim decided to produce his booklet in the shape of a heart. What do you think of his cover design?

Loving My Heart

READ
WRITE

As you have already collected your information, think about and write down
• a title for your booklet
• a shape for your booklet.
Now turn over and read Tim's finished booklet.

READ

Tim's finished booklet looked like this.

Contents

Introduction

The heart is the main organ of the body. It pumps the blood around the body. However, it can become damaged.

1

Eating Fat

Fat is one of the main risk factors in causing heart attacks. If a lot of fat is eaten the arteries may clog up with fat. The blood will not flow properly and a heart attack may happen.

FAT

2

Exercise

Lack of exercise may cause a heart attack. Being active is not only good for the circulation and heart, it also uses lots of calories and helps people lose weight.

9 Pounds

3

70

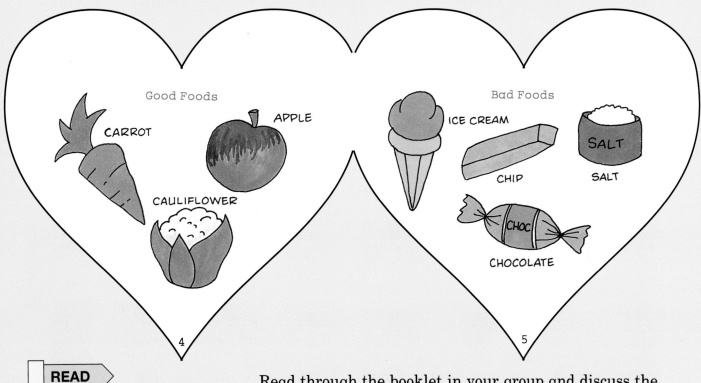

Good Foods

CARROT

APPLE

CAULIFLOWER

4

Bad Foods

ICE CREAM

CHIP

SALT

SALT

CHOC

CHOCOLATE

5

READ
TALK
WRITE

Read through the booklet in your group and discuss the following questions:

- Has Tim used Standard English for his booklet?
- If you were writing a booklet, would you use Standard English? Say why.
- Are you able to understand what Tim has written?
- How useful are his pictures?
- Could you have improved on Tim's booklet? If so, how?

Using the information you have collected, produce your own booklet.

Presenting information

Poem

Aim: learning how you can present information in a poem.

READ

In an acrostic poem, the first letter of each line spells what the poem is about.

Read these three poems, written by children who were researching information about creatures living in their pond. Instead of writing an information booklet like Tim's, they chose to put their information into acrostic poems.

Read these poems.

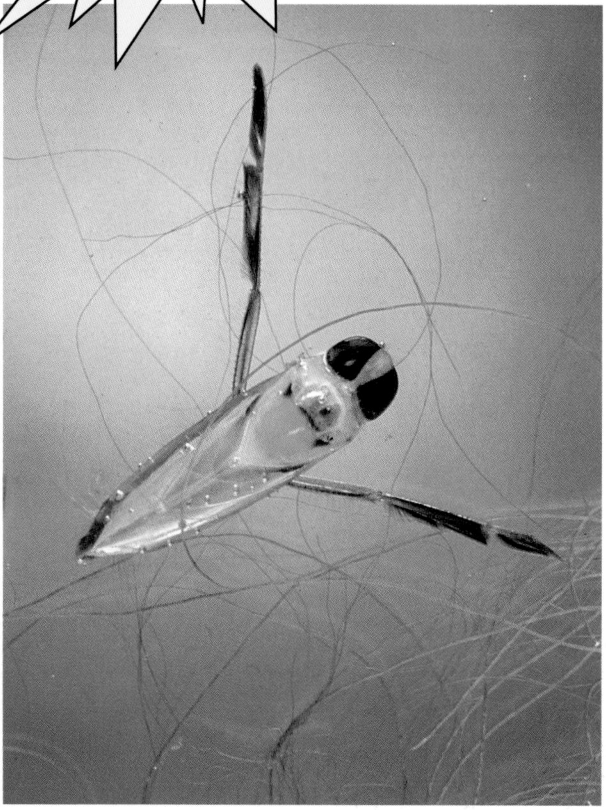

Water Boatman

Water boatman perfect swimmer.
Always showing itself above and
         flashing
                 down
                         again.
Turning and disappearing, popping up for air.
Eating its prey by sucking it.
Rests under the surface then stalks its prey.

Brilliant pale brown above dark under the water.
Oxygen is taken down on hairs on abdomen.
All eggs laid singly on water plants.
Terrifies every creature by its quick movements.
Male is short and fat with detailed skin.
Anchoring its feet in the mud to rest.
Never stopping its massive paddle-like feet.

Matthew Bevan

The Dragonfly

Delicate veins in his transparent wings,
Rarely rests on reeds,
Attacks flying insects,
Glossy skin any colour.
On his back are dots like jewels,
Nature gave him this gift.

From ghostly nymph to beautiful creature,
Living prince of the pond, king of the air,
Yet he is so delicate.

John Page

The Sludgeworm

Slimy, segmented sludgeworm
Lives on the bottom,
Under the mud,
Down below the surface,
Glowing red colour,
Earth volcanoes are its home.

Wet, wriggling water worms.
Oxygen absorbed by haemoglobin,
Reaching out with long bodies,
Massive masses of tangled worms.

Philip Smith, Thomas Morrissey, Helen Phillips
and Louise Bennett

READ ▷
WRITE ▷

Now check the information in **one** of these poems by looking in a reference book. Is everything correct?

Research an insect or animal which interests you, and write a similar poem.

Presenting information

Poster

Aim: *learning that we can present information in a poster.*

> **READ**

The extracts below are taken from a poster called 'Find Out About Fishing'. It was produced by The Angling Foundation.

Read these extracts carefully.

Brown trout. *Salmo trutta.*

Our native trout, distributed through-
out Britain in unpolluted rivers and in many lakes and reservoirs.

Size: British record: 8.880kg. Maximum size varies greatly with habitat.
In a small stream a brown trout of 500gm. is a good one; in a large reservoir,
loch (Scotland) or lough (Ireland) much bigger fish – 1 to 3 kg. – are
sometimes plentiful.

Artificial fly is usually the only permitted angling method, but there are
places where worm or spinning bait is allowed.

Perch.

Perca fluviatilis.

A boldly coloured, handsome
fish present throughout Britain in
rivers, lakes, canals and ponds,
and the first catch for many young
anglers. Note the spiny dorsal fin for protection
against predators, which include larger perch.

Size: British record: 2.523kg. For most anglers, a perch of 500gm.
is a welcome capture.

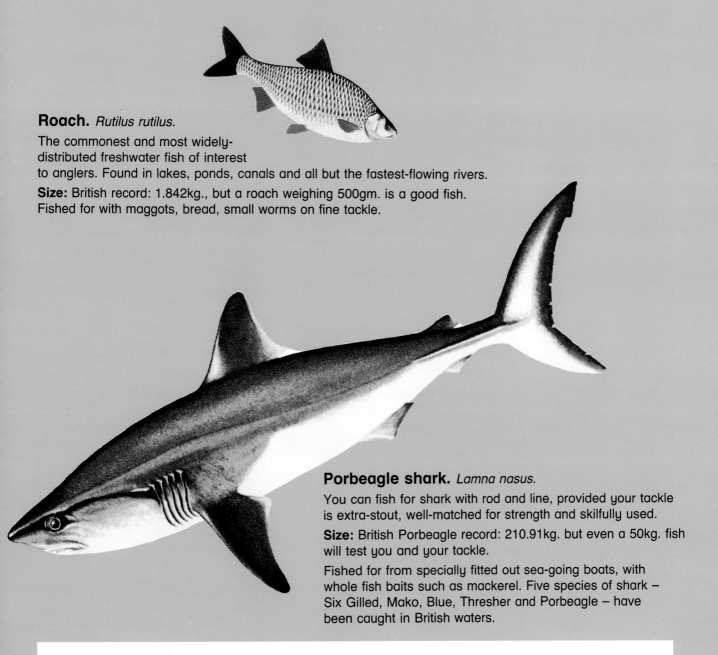

Roach. *Rutilus rutilus.*

The commonest and most widely-distributed freshwater fish of interest to anglers. Found in lakes, ponds, canals and all but the fastest-flowing rivers.

Size: British record: 1.842kg., but a roach weighing 500gm. is a good fish. Fished for with maggots, bread, small worms on fine tackle.

Porbeagle shark. *Lamna nasus.*

You can fish for shark with rod and line, provided your tackle is extra-stout, well-matched for strength and skilfully used.

Size: British Porbeagle record: 210.91kg. but even a 50kg. fish will test you and your tackle.

Fished for from specially fitted out sea-going boats, with whole fish baits such as mackerel. Five species of shark – Six Gilled, Mako, Blue, Thresher and Porbeagle – have been caught in British waters.

TALK
READ
WRITE

In pairs, first discuss and then write down:

1 Who do you think will read this poster?

2 What is the purpose of the poster?

3 How is the information presented (e.g. type of pictures, size of print, headings, the way it is written)?

4 Where might you see it?

5 Present some information which you have collected in a poster to go on your classroom wall.

Presenting information

Story

Aim: learning how writers and illustrators can present information through stories and pictures.

READ

Here is an extract from the book *Puffin* written by Naomi Lewis and illustrated by Deborah King. Naomi Lewis could have presented the information about puffins in a traditional information book with labelled diagrams, charts, and headings. Instead, she chose to write it as a story about one particular puffin called 'Puffin'. He is the main character in the book. We follow his life over a three year period which includes his migration to Newfoundland and his return. The book is packed with information about puffins.

Read the extract from the book below.

PUFFIN was born one Midsummer Day in an old rabbit burrow on an island off the northern coast of Scotland. Both parent birds had taken turns in guarding the egg for the five weeks before it hatched; now both worked hard to bring small fish to feed the little bird. In his dark nursery he was often alone, for puffins lay only one egg each season. But, outside, the air was filled with the noise of other sea-birds – guillemots, razor-bills, gannets, kittiwakes and other parent puffins like his own.

Here is the matching illustration by Deborah King. This beautiful picture is exactly like one you would expect to find in a story book.

Study this picture carefully.
1. Make a list of all the information you can find in the written passage.
2. Make a similar list of information you can find in the picture.
3. Write a story in which the main character is a bird or an animal. Find out as much information as you can about your creature before you start to write. Include all the information in your story, like Naomi Lewis has in her story called 'Puffin'.

Presenting information

News reporting

Aim: learning how to present information in a newspaper report.

One way of presenting information to many people is by publishing it in a newspaper. Journalists write about events which are news. Sometimes they are present at the scene of what is happening. We call this being an eyewitness. On other occasions journalists have to interview people to find out what happened.

READ

Read the following report about a shipwreck at sea. Notice how the reporter includes enough information to allow you, the reader, to picture what actually happened.

Eye-catching headline →

Attention-grabbing first sentence →

Time ↗

Place →

Name of boat ↗

People involved →

Rescue boat ←

Rescue aircraft ←

Boat which helped ←

Action taken ↖↙

Future plans ←

Crew saved as crabber sinks

A MAJOR resue operation was launched on Saturday morning when a Padstow fishing vessel radioed she was sinking off the North Cornwall coast.

The crabber, Pearn's Pride, was about six miles off Tintagel when water flooded her engine room.

Attempts by skipper Tony Comium and his crew to stem the leak failed and a Mayday signal was broadcast at about 0845. Flares were also sent up.

Padstow lifeboat was launched at 0900 and headed for the vessel which by that time was awash.

A helicopter was called out from RNAS Culdrose and the trawler Belle Anne, which was in the vicinity of the Pearn's Pride, joined in the rescue operation.

The Belle Anne went alongside the sinking crabber and took off crewmen Gordon Ballard and Rick Tavey while Mr Comium continued to pump water from his vessel.

When the vessel began to roll over, he stepped off and went aboard the Belle Anne.

Mr Comium and his crew were then transferred to the lifeboat and were taken to the boathouse on Trevose Head. Mr Comium later said he would try to raise the Pearn's Pride from its position 200 feet down.

News reports contain facts.

Before writing an article for the newspaper, the reporter would look at his or her notes. Read the notes below about another disaster at sea. Imagine that you are writing for a local newspaper. Write a short article based on the notes below. Present it in columns and think of a good headline.

Mystery object sinks 50ft. trawler named Quest.
2 warning flares – 11.20 p.m.
5 miles east of Hopes Nose – South Devon coast.
Alarm raised by P. Barczok (Teignmouth lifeboatman).
Lifeboat launched.
John Heddridge (42yrs) + Eddie Smith (43yrs) rescued from raft.
Taken to Brixham by Torbay lifeboat.
Mission Superintendent Paul Jarrett said men unhurt / kept in overnight.

TALK

WRITE

Compare your article with the journalist's report which was written for the Herald Express in Torquay. (Your teacher will find a copy of it in the Teacher's Book.) What have you written that is the same? What is different?

Now write a report for a school newspaper about things that are happening in your school or neighbourhood. You might need to interview people to get the facts.

Think of an eye-catching headline to go with your report.

Acknowledgements

We are grateful for permission to reproduce the following copyright material:

Dennis Hamley: from *Dangleboots* (Deutsch, 1987) by permission of Scholastic Publications Ltd.; **Edith Holden:** from *Country Diary of an Edwardian Lady* (Michael Joseph/Webb and Bower, 1977) © Richard Webb Ltd. 1977, by permission of Michael Joseph; **Ted Hughes:** from *How the Whale Became and Other Stories* (1963), by permission of the publishers, Faber & Faber Ltd.; **Laurie Lee:** from *Cider With Rosie* (Hogarth Press, 1959), and **Naomi Lewis:** from *Puffin* (Cape, 1984) illustrated by Deborah King, both by permission of Random House UK Ltd.; **Kit Wright:** 'Song of the Whale' from *Hot Dog and Other Poems* (Viking Kestrel and Puffin Books, 1981), © Kit Wright 1981, by permission of Penguin Books Ltd; and **Martyn Wiley:** 'The Hamster's Diary', from *The Hamster's Diary and Other Kinds of Writing* (Oxford University Press, 1992) © Martyn Wiley 1992, by permission of the author.

We are also grateful to the following whose work is first published here, all by permission of the authors: **Jessica Batten:** 'Pip's Diary', © Jessica Batten 1993; **Matthew Bevan:** 'Water Boatman', © Matthew Bevan 1993; **Sara Currie:** Otter letter, © Sara Currie 1993; **Trevor Harvey:** 'Beans' advertisement, © Trevor Harvey 1993; **Tim Hayes:** Heart booklet, © Tim Hayes 1993; **John Page:** 'The Dragonfly', © John Page 1993; and **Philip Smith, Thomas Morrissey, Helen Phillips,** and **Louise Bennett:** 'The Sludgeworm', © Philip Smith, Thomas Morrissey, Helen Phillips, and Louise Bennett 1993.

We would also like to thank:
The Angling Foundation for extracts from their poster, *Find Out About Fishing* (copies of the full poster and detailed angling information packs are available from The Angling Foundation, 23 Brighton Road, South Croydon, CR2 6AE); Beaucards Ridgeway for two greetings cards; the Bristol Old Vic for the *Aladdin* poster, produced by Marc Vyvyan-Jones; the Cornish Guardian for their article; and Times Newspapers Ltd/Rapho Photographic Agency and Network for the photograph by Hans Sylvester on the front cover of the *Sunday Times Magazine*, © Times Newspapers Ltd, 1989.

Although every effort has been made to trace and contact copyright holders before publication, this has not been possible in some cases. We apologise for any apparent infringement of copyright and will be pleased to rectify any omissions at the earliest opportunity.

Acknowledgements for Oxford Primary English Book 4

Photographs: The Duke of Beaufort p.62 (bottom); Andrew Besley p.78; Bruce Coleman Ltd pp.72–73 (all); The Environmental Picture Library p.23 (4); Paul Glendell p.22 (1); Sally and Richard Greenhill p.46; Greenpeace pp.22–23 (2, 3, and 5); The Hutchison Library p.46; Rob Judges pp.25, 32, 46, 47, 79 (all); Tristram Kenton pp. 31, 48 (all); The Kobal Collection p.46; The Master and Fellows, Magdalen College, Cambridge p.62 (script); The National Gallery p.50; The National Portrait Gallery p.62 (top); Rex Features p.46; Sporting Pictures (UK) Ltd p.46.

The illustrations are by: Jane Bottomley pp.4, 5, 6, 7, 57 (top right); Juliet Breese pp.55, 56–57; Martin Chatterton p.11 (bottom); Gerard Gibson pp.51–54; Michael Hingley p.65; David Holmes pp.28–29; Antony Lee pp.26–27; Alan Marks p.13; Nilesh Mistry pp.36–45; David Mitcheson p.30; Chris Molan p.16; Jane Ormes pp.18–20; Nicki Palin pp.14–16; Chris Price p.9; Julie Roberts pp.10, 11 (top); Caroline Sharpe pp.34–35; and Renée Williams pp.20, 47, 66, 67, 71 (top).

The handwriting and illustrations on pp. 5, 7, 9, 17, 23, 27, 29, 35, 57, 68, 69, 70, 71, and 79 are by Elitta Fell.